All About Animals

Tigers

By Christina Wilsdon

Reader's Digest Young Families

Contents

Chapter 1
A Tiger Story

Baby Tiger huddled quietly next to his sister in the tall grass beside their den. The two little tigers wished they could play. But Mama Tiger had gone hunting for food. Although they were only a few weeks old, the little cubs already knew it was not safe to play without Mama Tiger to guard them. So they lay still, waiting for her to come back.

Suddenly they saw the tall grass shake. Something was coming. Was it a hungry hyena or a wild dog? Baby Tiger crouched low. Then he heard a noise that sounded like "chuff, chuff"—a tiger's way of saying hello!

Baby Tiger and his sister ran out of their hiding place. They rubbed against Mama Tiger's face. She licked them all over with her big washcloth of a tongue.

Then Mama Tiger flopped down on her side and stretched out. Baby Tiger and his sister settled beside her to drink the warm milk that Mama Tiger's body made for them.

When Baby Tiger and his sister were eight weeks old, Mama Tiger started sharing some of her own meals with them. One day she dragged home the leg bone of a deer. Baby Tiger and his sister gnawed on it and nibbled at the meat. They liked this new treat!

Mama Tiger lay down near the cubs and watched over them as they ate. Baby Tiger walked over to her when he was done. He jumped onto the tip of her twitching tail. She pushed him over with her big paw and licked his face clean.

The next day Mama Tiger decided it was time to move her cubs to a new den. She picked up Baby Tiger by the scruff of his neck with her mouth. This did not hurt a bit. Baby Tiger simply relaxed and went limp as a rag doll while Mama Tiger carried him to their new home. Then she went back for his sister.

Baby Tiger grew bigger and stronger. By the time he was four months old, he followed Mama Tiger wherever she went. Baby Tiger and his sister even tagged after Mama Tiger when she went hunting.

Following Mama Tiger through the grass was fun. But the two little cubs did not like lying still and silent as Mama sneaked up on a deer. The two little cubs nipped at each other and started to play. They forgot to be quiet.

The cubs' squeaks and growls scared away the prey. This made Mama Tiger very angry. She growled at her naughty cubs and swatted them with her paw.

Tiger Moms

A mother tiger gives birth to two or three cubs at a time. Cubs may be born in a den among rocks or tree roots. A mother tiger may also give birth in a patch of tall grass.

Wild Words

A female tiger is called a tigress. *Her babies are called* cubs.

Tiger Babies

Tiger cubs weigh only two to three pounds at birth. At first they are blind and deaf. They can open their eyes when they are two weeks old.

In time, the cubs learned to watch and wait patiently. Soon they did not even move a whisker until after Mama Tiger caught her prey. Then they rushed to join her. She always stood back to let the cubs eat first.

Baby Tiger and his sister stopped drinking Mama Tiger's milk when they were about six months old. Now they were like Mama Tiger—they ate only meat. They also learned to hunt like Mama Tiger.

The two cubs had been watching her hunt for a long time. At first, they hunted small animals. They sneaked up on monkeys and young deer. Sometimes they even caught them.

Baby Tiger and his sister got better at hunting as they grew. Some days they went off on their own to explore and to hunt. But they still needed to be with Mama Tiger so they could learn more.

By the time Baby Tiger and his sister turned two years old, they were nearly all grown up. Mama Tiger soon stopped sharing her food with them. They really did not need her to watch out for them anymore.

One day, Baby Tiger went out to explore on his own, and he did not come back. He kept traveling, hoping to find a mate. His sister also left Mama Tiger and found a place to live nearby. Someday, one of them might take over the land where Mama Tiger roamed.

Chapter 2

The Body of a Tiger

A tiger can leap 30 feet in just one bound. That is nearly the length of a school bus! A tiger can also jump 15 feet straight up – high enough to peek into a second-story window!

Here, Kitty, Kitty!

A tiger is a big cat—a very big cat! It is the largest member of the cat family, a group that includes house cats and lions. A male tiger can measure 9 feet long from its pink nose to the tip of its tail. It can weigh about 600 pounds.

Imagine if a kitty this size took a nap on your couch. It would be as long—or longer—than the couch. And it would weigh five to six times as much!

Paws and Claws

Look at a cat's paws, and you will see that each one has four big toes. A small fifth toe sits above each of its front paws. A tiger's paws look the same—just a lot bigger! Its paw can measure up to 12 inches wide. Look at a 12-inch ruler and imagine a tiger paw covering it!

Soft pads on the bottoms of a tiger's paws help it walk quietly as it sneaks up on prey. Lurking inside these big, soft paws are sharp, strong claws. The claws are hidden inside the tiger's furry toes when the tiger walks or runs. This keeps the claws from getting worn down. The claws come out when the tiger stretches its paws to grip prey or defend itself.

Tiger Teeth

The four big teeth you see in a tiger's mouth are called canine teeth. They can measure 4 inches long—nearly as long as a one dollar bill! These teeth are used to kill prey.

The tiger also has 26 other teeth. The front teeth between its fangs are used for nibbling and grooming. The back teeth have sharp, knifelike edges for slicing meat from bones.

Tiger Senses

Most tigers have golden eyes. Keen eyesight helps them hunt in the dim light of dawn and dusk. Tigers also hunt at night. Their eyes glow in the dark when light shines on them. They glow because the light is reflected off a layer of cells in the back of each eye. The reflected light helps tigers to see even better in the dark.

A tiger's ears swivel to catch sound from all directions. Its sharp hearing helps it listen for prey. Its sensitive nose picks up the scent of prey as well as that of other tigers. Whiskers on its muzzle help it sense the size and shape of nearby objects.

Roar!

A tiger's roar can be heard up to 2 miles away. Tigers roar both to find mates and to warn other tigers to stay away. Tigers also hiss, spit, growl, snarl, moan, meow, and chuff. A chuff is a huffing noise made through the nose.

The tiger's four big teeth are the largest biting teeth of any land predator. A tiger can kill its prey with just one bite!

Fun Fact

The tiger is the only wild cat with stripes!

A tiger has from 100 to 150 stripes. Different types of tigers have different numbers of stripes.

Stripe Types

Every tiger has its own special pattern of stripes that is different from any other tiger's pattern—just as your fingers have their own special set of fingerprints. Some stripes are solid lines. Some stripes are made up of two lines joined at both ends with a patch of color in between. Some stripes may be rows of spots.

Spot the Tiger

An orange tiger with black stripes looks bold and bright. But its coloring helps the animal blend in with its surroundings, by breaking up the shape of its body. When the sun shines through tall grass and trees, it creates patterns of light and dark. The tiger's stripy coat helps the animal blend in with the streaks of sunshine and shadow. This blending-in is called camouflage, and it keeps tigers hidden as they sneak up on their prey.

Eyespots on Ears!

A tiger has a big white spot on the back of each ear called an eyespot. Scientists think eyespots help tigers and other cats use their ears to "talk" to one another. An angry tiger, for example, flattens its ears so the back part faces forward. The eyespots may make it easier for one tiger to "read" another tiger's ears—even from far away—just as our eyebrows help us signal thoughts and feelings.

Chapter 3

Tigers on the Prowl

If it is hunting by a water hole, a tiger will chase its prey into the water to slow it down.

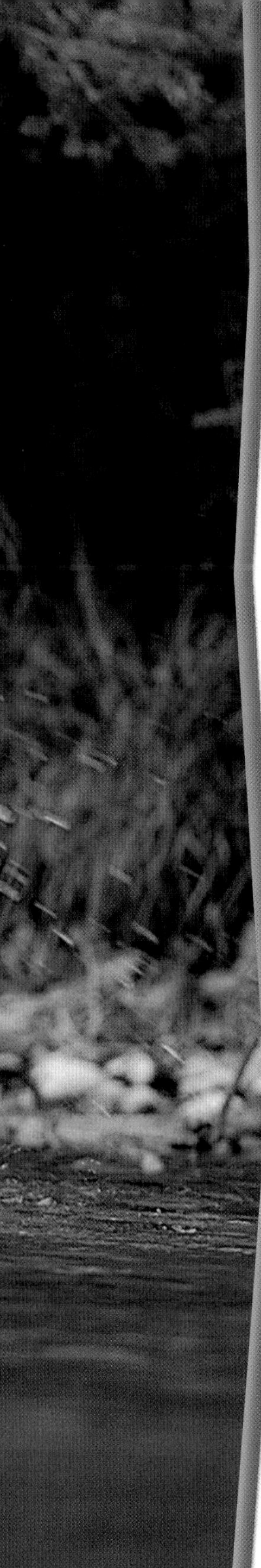

Surprise Attack

A tiger hunts by stealth. Slowly, quietly, it sneaks up on its prey. It crouches low so that its belly almost rubs the ground. Without a sound, it creeps forward. It may even circle around its prey again and again, moving closer each time. It hides behind plants and rocks as it moves. This way of hunting is called stalking.

The tiger does not attack until it is about 30 feet from its prey. That distance is about three times its own body length. The tiger bursts from its hiding place and bounds toward its prey in mighty leaps.

But even now, the prey may get away. A tiger can run at full speed for only a short distance. Just one hunt out of every twenty ends successfully with a meal for the tiger.

The tiger attacks by grabbing the prey from behind or from the side with its huge front paws. It hangs on with its claws. The struggle ends with a bite to the back of the neck or the throat.

A Tiger Menu

The tiger is a meat eater—a carnivore. It eats deer, wild pigs, and even large wild cattle such as water buffalo. Sometimes it will even try to catch a baby rhinoceros. A tiger will also eat small animals such as insects, fish, and birds if it can't find larger prey.

Cat Food

A hungry tiger drags its prey to a safe spot to eat. This safe spot may be deep among plants or in the water. A tiger is strong enough to drag a meal heavier than itself for as much as a quarter of a mile! That's about the length of five city streets.

Then the tiger settles down to eat. It may swallow 45 pounds of meat in just one night—enough to make 180 quarter-pound hamburgers! A big tiger that is very hungry may gobble as much as 90 pounds of meat in one night.

Leftovers

A tiger uses its paws to scrape leaves over what is left of its meal to hide it. The tiger comes back to feed on the leftovers until all the meat is gone.

A tiger does not need to hunt every day. It may catch prey just once a week. In a year, a tiger may eat about 45 deer. A tigress with cubs needs up to 70 meals a year.

R-r-r-rough!

Have you ever been licked by a cat? A cat's tongue is rough, like sandpaper. So is a tiger's tongue. The tongue is rough enough to scrape meat from bones as the tiger feeds.

Tigers lick their fur clean after they are done eating.

Tigers who are mates
spend time playing
and chasing each other.

Keep Out!

A tiger normally lives and hunts by itself. It roams a large area of land, padding along trails that wind through forests and plains. This area of land is called a tiger's home range. A tiger's range includes its territory—a place that a tiger protects from other tigers. The territory may be the size of the home range or just a part of it.

A tiger warns other tigers away from its territory by marking it with signs that say "No Trespassing!" Most of these marks are meant to be smelled. A tiger sprays urine on tree trunks and rocks to leave its scent. Its feet also leave scent wherever the animal steps. The tiger also scratches trunks to leave scent on them as well as big scratch marks.

Two's Company

Tigers growl at trespassers on their territory. The trespasser usually leaves without a fight. Sometimes two tigers wrestle and bite before one of them finally leaves.

But when a tigress is ready to mate, she does not chase male tigers away. She marks her territory to attract them instead. She may even leave her territory to look for a mate.

After the tigress finds a mate, the two big cats play together as if they were cubs again. But the male leaves long before the baby tigers are born. The tigress does not need or want his help in raising them.

Chapter 4
Types of Tigers

Some Bengal tigers are white with dark brown stripes. Some have blue eyes.

White Tigers

White Bengal tigers are sometimes born in the wild, but they rarely survive. Their color does not help them blend in with their habitat. White tigers are often found in zoos and circuses.

Six Types of Tigers

Six different types of tigers exist today. They all belong to the same species. Each separate kind is called a subspecies. The subspecies are different from each other and live in different places.

Bengal Tigers

The Bengal tiger is the most common subspecies. It is sometimes called the royal tiger or Indian tiger, and it is the national symbol of India. Most Bengal tigers live in India. Small populations also live in Myanmar, Bangladesh, Nepal, Bhutan, and China.

Bold black stripes run up and down the Bengal tiger's coat. Its color ranges from golden orange to the deep orange of a flame. A ruff of fur surrounds its face.

Bengal tigers live in thick woods and among tall grasses. They often flop into water holes and rivers to cool off. They are good swimmers, too.

In 1900, many thousands of Bengal tigers lived in the wild. Today there are between 3,000 and 5,000 of them. The government of India protects its tigers and sets aside land for them called tiger reserves.

Siberian Tigers

The Siberian tiger gets its name from where it lives—Siberia. Siberia is a vast land of forests and plains that spreads across most of Russia. Siberia is known for its long, cold winters and snowy landscapes. A tiger from a warm, tropical place could not survive in Siberia. But the Siberian tiger is perfectly at home in this wintry land.

One adaptation is its large size. A male can weigh up to 660 pounds and sometimes even more. Large animals lose less body heat to the air around them for their size than a small animal does. A layer of fat under the skin helps keep this tiger warm, too.

The Siberian tiger's coat is also adapted for life in the cold. Its tawny fur is paler than the coats of tropical tigers, blending in with its habitat of snow and forest. It has fewer stripes than other kinds of tigers. Its fur is also longer, especially on its neck, back, and underside. In winter, the Siberian tiger grows an extra-thick coat.

Just half a century ago, there were only 40 to 50 Siberian tigers left in the wild. Laws were passed to stop tiger hunting. Russia's government has also worked to save areas of forest from being cut down so that the tigers have places to live. Today, there are about 300 to 400 wild Siberian tigers.

Extinct Tigers

Three kinds of tigers have gone extinct in the past 60 years. They are the Bali tiger, the Caspian tiger, and the Javan tiger.

The Siberian tiger is the
biggest kind of tiger.

There are only 300 to 400 Sumatran tigers that live in the wild today.

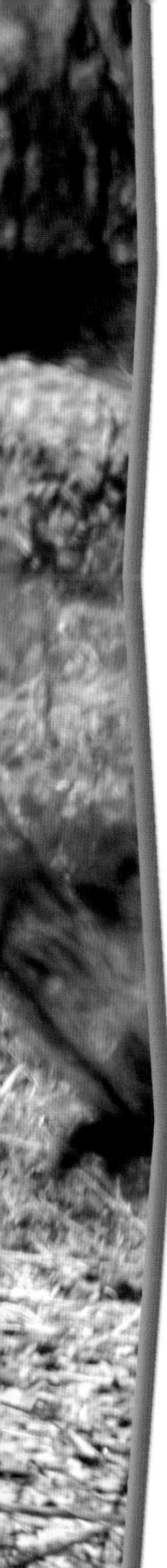

Sumatran Tigers

The Sumatran tiger lives on the island of Sumatra in the Indian Ocean. This island is part of the nation of Indonesia.

The Sumatran tiger is the smallest kind of tiger. A male Sumatran tiger is up to 8 feet long and weighs about 300 pounds—about as much as two average people. Its smaller size helps it slink easily through jungles thick with plants.

Stripes help camouflage this tropical tiger. And the Sumatran has stripes to spare! It has more stripes than any other subspecies of tiger. Its fur is also darker. The male also has the longest furry ruff around its face.

Three More Tigers

The three other tiger subspecies are the Indochinese tiger, South China tiger, and the Malayan tiger.

Indochinese tigers live in Thailand and some other nearby countries. Their stripes sometimes appear as rows of spots!

The South China tiger is the subspecies that scientists think is most like the original ancestor of tigers. There are fewer than 40 of these tigers left in the wild.

The Malayan tiger is a "new" kind of tiger that was discovered in 2004. They used to be part of the same group as Indochinese tigers. But scientists who studied the two kinds of tigers found lots of small differences between them. They decided the Malayan tiger was a separate subspecies.

Chapter 5
Tigers in the World

Where Tigers Live

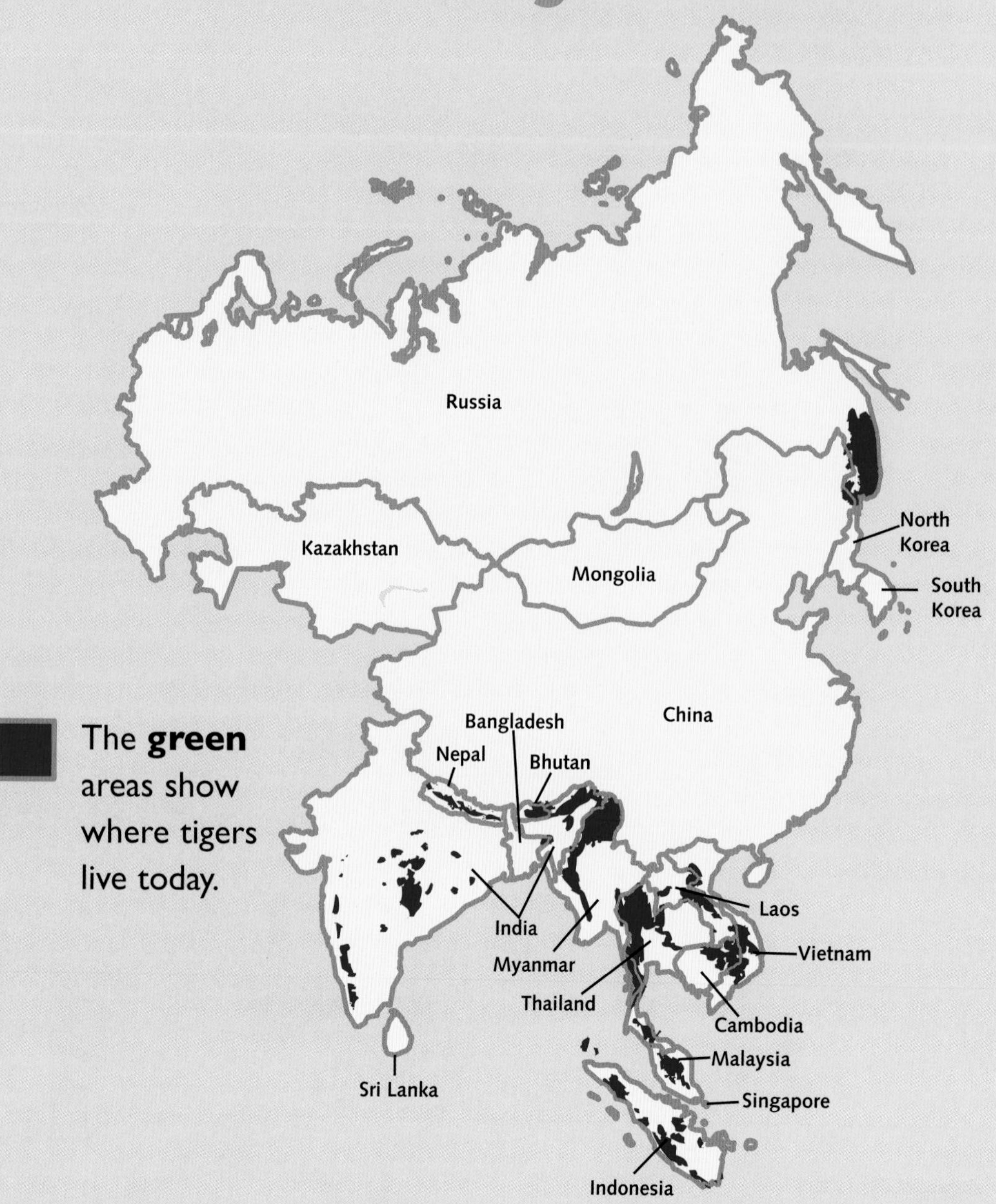

The **green** areas show where tigers live today.

Different types of tigers live in different parts of Asia. But all tigers live in habitats that have forests, areas of water, and large prey to hunt. The Siberian tiger lives in forests in cold, snowy places. Other types of tigers live in tropical rain forests. Almost half of the tigers' habitat has disappeared in the last 10 years because people have cut down forests for farms and houses.

Tigers and People

People and tigers share a history that goes back thousands of years. Early humans both feared tigers and admired their strength. People were often the prey of these powerful predators. Over time, weapons such as spears were invented and used to protect people and their cattle. People also used their weapons to hunt and became the tiger's only predator.

Tiger hunting became a sport in parts of Asia. Powerful rulers went on tiger hunts. About 150 years ago, people from Europe began going to Asia to hunt tigers, too.

Tiger Hunting Today

Tigers are now protected by laws in many places. But illegal hunting, called poaching, still goes on.

Poachers kill tigers to sell their skins and body parts. The striped skins are turned into rugs and wall hangings. The rest of the tiger is sold for jewelry, good-luck charms, and other products. Some people believe the tiger's strength will protect them and make them healthy and strong.

The Future of Tigers

Poaching and habitat loss are the two biggest threats to the survival of tigers. Many forests have been cut down in Asia and turned into farmland over the past 100 years. Tigers have fewer places to live and less to eat. Today, there are only about 6,000 tigers in the wild. This number may grow with efforts to save tigers and their habitat.

Fast Facts About Bengal Tigers

Scientific name	*Panthera tigris tigris*
Class	Mammalia
Order	Carnivora
Size	Males up to 10 feet in length including tail Females up to 9 feet in length including tail
Weight	Males to 660 pounds Females to 350 pounds
Life span	15 years in the wild 20 years in captivity
Habitat	Forests, swamps
Top speed	About 35 miles per hour

Saving the Tigers

In the early 1900s, there were about 100,000 tigers living in the wild. By 1960, there were only about 2,500 of these big cats. Projects such as special tiger reserves in India that have guards who keep out poachers have been successful in helping to keep tigers from becoming extinct.

Glossary of Wild Words

camouflage colors and patterns on an animal that help it blend in with its surroundings

carnivore an animal that eats meat

chuff a huffing noise made through the nose

conservation the protection and preservation of land, animals, plants, and other natural resources

cub a baby tiger

eyespot the white spot on the back of a tiger's ear

genus a large category of related plants or animals consisting of smaller groups (species) of closely related plants or animals

poaching illegal hunting

predator an animal that hunts and eats other animals to survive

prey animals that are hunted by other animals for food

range all the places where a species lives

reserves areas of land or water where wildlife and plants are protected

species a group of living things that are the same in many ways

stalking sneaking up on an animal while hunting

subspecies a group of living things in a species that are similar to one another but different from other members of that species

territory an area of land that an animal considers to be its own and will fight to defend

tigress a female tiger

trespassing entering a territory that belongs to another without permission

Index